CAREERS THAT COUNT

HUMANITARIAN AID WORKER

Louise Spilsbury

PowerKiDS
press.

New York

Published in 2016 by **The Rosen Publishing Group**
29 East 21st Street, New York, NY 10010

Produced for Rosen by Calcium

Editors for Calcium: Sarah Eason and Jennifer Sanderson
Designer: Emma DeBanks

Picture credits: Cover: Shutterstock: American Spirit (bottom), Northfoto (top); Inside:
Dreamstime: Antonella865 23, Gillespaire 16–17, Mares Lucian 20–21, Steve Mann 17t,
Photographerlondon 22, David Snyder 21r; Shutterstock: American Spirit 7, ChameleonsEye
15, Chris Dorney 2, Charlie Edward 25, Vlad Galenko 4, Sadik Gulec 4–5; 27, A Katz 10–11,
Kojoku 18–19, Vasiliy Koval 8r, Sura Nualpradid 26, Snig 27, Tashatuvango 1b, 28, Tracing Tea
9, A. S. Zain 12–13, 14–15, 24.

Cataloging-in-Publication Data
Spilsbury, Louise.
Humanitarian aid worker / by Louise Spilsbury.
p. cm. — (Careers that count)
Includes index.
ISBN 978-1-4994-0801-0 (pbk.)
ISBN 978-1-4994-0800-3 (6 pack)
ISBN 978-1-4994-0799-0 (library binding)
1. Humanitarian assistance — Juvenile literature.
2. Disaster relief — Juvenile literature. I. Spilsbury, Louise. II. Title.
HV553.S65 2016
363.34'8023—d23

Manufactured in the United States of America
CPSIA Compliance Information: Batch WS15PK: For Further Information contact Rosen Publishing, New York, New York at 1-800-237-9932

CONTENTS

WHICH CAREERS COUNT?

Do you know what job you would like to do when you are older? What matters most to you about the kind of work you might do? People choose their careers for a variety of different reasons. Most of us would like a job that is interesting and challenging, but some people want more than that. They want a career that counts. Careers that count are those that make a real difference in other people's lives, such being a police officer, search and rescue pilot, or firefighter.

Challenging Careers

Careers that count can be challenging, difficult, and sometimes dangerous. However, the people who do these jobs love their work because they get a huge sense of satisfaction from helping others. Some people work to save lives, solve crimes, or rescue people from danger. In this book we will look at the work of emergency humanitarian aid workers. These are people who help those who are in real need. They work to improve the lives of those who are poor, in danger, or in other difficulties in countries **abroad**.

Aid workers help people in different ways, from delivering food to providing schools.

Humanitarian aid workers help people in desperate need all over the world.

Careers That Count: A Career for You?

How do people choose the right career? They start by figuring out the answers to basic questions like these.

- What are they good at? What do they like doing? What do other people say they are good at?
- Do they like being outdoors or inside? Do they like to work with people or alone?
- What do they know about the sorts of jobs they might like to do? Reading this book is a good place to start.

HEROES ABROAD

Humanitarian aid workers do one of the most worthwhile of jobs. They are trained to help people who face life-threatening challenges in countries all over the world. Aid workers travel to dangerous places during **natural disasters** like floods and earthquakes, to help people who are injured or have no water. They help people find food and **shelter** when they have had to leave their homes because of war. They help people get the equipment they need to make a living when they have lost their livelihoods.

Doctors use their medical training to become aid workers who treat people who are sick and in need.

WHAT MAKES A GREAT HUMANITARIAN AID WORKER?

Humanitarian aid workers are trained to do their jobs. However, it is a challenging job in which situations can change overnight. As well as training, aid workers need certain **characteristics** to be able to carry out their job well. Humanitarian aid workers must be:

- Caring: humanitarian aid workers put the needs of others before their own.

- **Adaptable**: they need to be able to adjust to new conditions.

- Quick to learn: when they are placed in a new area with new problems, aid workers have to learn quickly.

Which of the above do you think is most important and why?

Careers That Count: Becoming a Humanitarian Aid Worker

Humanitarian aid workers need to have a university or college degree. The type of work they do may depend on the type of degree they have. Many aid workers study **sociology** or **economic development**. Medical aid workers need a medical degree. Aid workers also need experience in working for **charities** or other aid organizations.

IN THE OFFICE

When people think of aid workers, they often think of them traveling around exciting places in faraway countries. This does happen, but the truth is that many aid workers spend a lot of time in offices, either in their home country or abroad.

There are a lot of important decisions that aid workers must make. Aid workers attend meetings to discuss plans, how to apply for or spend money, or how to help people. They have to figure out budgets for the projects they are working on and write reports about their work for **headquarters**. They also have office meetings with people from **communities** where they work, to find out what people need and how they think the aid worker could best help them.

Careers That Count: Working with Budgets

Different aid workers do different types of work, but many have to create or work with budgets. Budgets are calculations about how much money is needed to do something and how much should be spent on different parts of that job. That is why many aid workers need training or experience with money and computers, to be able to handle budgets well.

People think being an aid worker is all about adventure, but aid workers also have to do a lot of paperwork.

Aid workers spend a lot of time in meetings finding out what kind of aid could help communities.

WHAT MAKES A GREAT HUMANITARIAN AID WORKER?

Humanitarian aid workers need to be patient. It can take a long time to get the funding or help that is needed to make projects work. How do you think being patient can help aid workers deal with the months, or even years, of office-based work it can take to get a **development** project started?

DISASTER RELIEF

Humanitarian aid workers help people in all kinds of disaster situations. They help people who have been injured or have no food or shelter because of floods, earthquakes, and hurricanes. When a disaster hits an area, especially in a poor country, many people are affected and help is needed immediately.

Careers That Count: Taking the Lead

Some aid workers do not hand out food parcels or aid directly. They organize **volunteers** to do this work. For example, they organize the delivery of food supplies, the trucks necessary to deliver that food, and the volunteers to drive those trucks to where they are needed. They make sure those volunteers know exactly where to go and how to distribute the aid when they arrive there.

When aid workers arrive at the site of a disaster, their first job is to quickly figure out what needs to be done first. Some aid workers give medical treatment to people who are injured. Other aid workers **distribute** emergency supplies, such as blankets, clothing, food, and water. Some try to help those who have been separated from their families find their loved ones.

It takes a lot of organization to make sure aid is fairly shared and distributed to where it is most needed.

WHAT MAKES A GREAT HUMANITARIAN AID WORKER?

In a disaster situation, aid workers have to work closely with other emergency departments, such as firefighters and police officers. They also deal with local staff who work for aid agencies, and volunteers from the local community. How do you think being a good team player, someone who works well with others, helps aid workers do a good job?

MEDICAL AID

There are aid workers all over the world who are trained doctors and nurses. They can deliver medical assistance to people who need it quickly.

Medical aid workers run **clinics** in poor areas of the world. These clinics mean that people can drop in for free and get treatment for themselves or their families. Medical aid workers also carry out **vaccinations** to stop people from getting dangerous diseases in the future. After a disaster, medical aid workers travel to the affected area and set up **temporary** hospitals, with beds and equipment, so they can start treating the wounded immediately. Medical aid workers may also work in **war zones**, treating injured soldiers from both sides of the battle.

By giving this baby a vaccination, this aid worker will save him from catching a life-threatening disease in the future.

WHAT MAKES A GREAT HUMANITARIAN AID WORKER?

Aid workers have to be adaptable. When working abroad they may have to **diagnose** and treat medical conditions not often found where they live. They may have to work without the equipment they have at home. How do you think being able to adjust to new conditions quickly can help medical aid workers do their job?

Careers That Count: Medical Training

People must be fully qualified as doctors, nurses, or **specialists** in particular diseases before they can become medical aid workers. Most aid agencies and charities also require aid workers to have been working in a hospital or clinic for at least six months within the two-year period before they become medical aid workers. This ensures that the medical aid workers are up to date with modern medical methods.

DISASTER PREVENTION

Little can be done to prevent natural disasters, but aid workers can train people to be better prepared for when they do happen.

Some aid workers help communities organize early warning systems for people in areas of danger. This gives them time to move away from the area before the disaster happens. Aid workers also build shelters where people can stay during events like hurricanes. Some workers train local people in **first aid** so they are ready to help people injured if a disaster happens. This also means people will be ready to help themselves if and when they are faced with another emergency.

When local people have first aid skills, they can treat people in their community themselves.

Careers That Count: Keeping Healthy

Aid workers visit areas where there may be disease, dirty water, and other things that can make them sick. It is important that they see a specialist to get **vaccines**, medicines, and advice on how to stay safe and healthy while they are traveling. They should also visit their own doctor before they leave home, to make sure they are physically fit for the demands of the job. They should also have a checkup when they return.

After a disaster, some aid workers find out what people need to help them prepare for future disasters.

WHAT MAKES A GREAT HUMANITARIAN AID WORKER?

Aid workers often travel far from home and may be away for nine months or more at a time. They may stay in places without regular electricity supplies, which means they may not be able to make contact with people at home very often. What **sacrifices** do you think aid workers may have to make in their personal lives to have careers that count?

SANITATION

Clean water is something many of us take for granted, but providing a community with water and **sanitation** is one of the most important ways to keep people healthy.

Some aid workers teach local people about diseases that can be passed on in dirty water, and the importance of washing their hands. These people can then return to their communities and teach others about the importance of good sanitation. Some aid workers work with communities to build wells or **water pumps**, to bring supplies of freshwater to a village. This also saves children and others from having to walk miles every day to fetch water.

Providing a community with a supply of clean water is one of the most important ways of helping them keep healthy.

Technical aid workers are trained to do things like figure out how much water a community needs. They are also trained to figure out where, and how, it is best to drill a well or water pump. They know which materials to use to make a well or water pump. They are also trained to teach local people how to build the pumps and wells, and how to maintain and mend them.

Aid workers' technical skills can be vital in helping to complete a sanitation project.

WHAT MAKES A GREAT HUMANITARIAN AID WORKER?

It is important for aid workers to listen to what communities want. Aid workers must find out all they can about an area and its **resources** from local people. For example, local people may know the best place to build a well. How do you think being a good **communicator**, being able to pass on and take in information quickly and clearly, helps an aid worker achieve the best results?

17

HELPING REFUGEES

Refugees are people who have had to leave their country, often because of war, and are too afraid to return. Aid workers help refugees in different ways.

When refugees first **flee** their homes, they may escape to a place where they have no food or shelter. Aid workers deliver tents, blankets, kitchen sets, baby packs, and medicines. Refugees may have to live in tents for a long time before they find a new home, so aid workers continue to help them there. Aid workers try to find homes for the refugees in other countries. They also help the refugees get money or jobs, to help them survive when they first arrive in a new country.

Careers That Count: Paperwork

Aid workers must learn how to fill out forms, **applications**, and other types of paperwork to be able to ask for **financial** and other forms of help for refugees. Paperwork is also needed to **reunite** refugees with missing family members, and to help refugees find a permanent place to live.

18

Keeping records of what refugees have and need is a vital part of some aid workers' jobs.

WHAT MAKES A GREAT HUMANITARIAN AID WORKER?

It can be very difficult to organize help for large numbers of people at a refugee camp, or victims of a natural disaster. Things often go wrong or do not go as planned. Aid workers must be determined: they must have a strong feeling that they will get something done, no matter what. How do you think this can help aid workers keep working in difficult situations?

FAMINE RELIEF

Famines happen when an area has an extreme shortage of food. They usually take place in countries where there are **droughts** that cause **crops** to die and farm animals to **starve**. These countries are often very poor, so they do not have the money to buy enough food to feed people during a famine.

When there is no rain, plants die. Without plants to feed themselves or their animals, people go hungry, too.

WHAT MAKES A GREAT HUMANITARIAN AID WORKER?

Aid workers need to be tough. It can be very upsetting seeing people, and especially small children, who are starving to death. Why do you think is it important for aid workers to be both caring but also not overly affected by other people's suffering?

Aid workers provide famine relief in different ways. Some aid workers work in their home countries where they make up boxes of food supplies to send out to areas of famine. Others figure out how much food is needed per person and where to send it. Aid workers can fly or drive the food boxes to where they are needed, or help distribute them. They also treat people, especially children, for malnutrition. This is when people have had so little food they are very sick and may be starving to death.

Deliveries of food are vital when an area is suffering a famine.

Careers That Count: Dealing with Malnutrition

Aid workers working in famine situations are trained to know when a child has severe malnutrition. These children are very thin because their bodies have used most of their fat and muscle for energy, in order to stay alive. Aid workers must give the children special, high-energy food to help them get well. They must also give them medicines to treat any **infections**.

DEVELOPMENT PROJECTS

Development projects are those that help people in developing countries figure out long-term solutions to problems. Most people want to be able to care for themselves and their own communities, so aid workers try to find ways of helping them do this.

Aid workers meet with people to find out how to help them become **self-sufficient**. They might organize and supply farm equipment to help people start up farms. They may organize **loans** of money to help people start up, or rebuild, businesses. Some aid workers train people in new skills, so they are able to deal with future challenges. Others provide materials and teach local people how to build bridges and roads. New bridges and roads make it easier for people to travel, which helps them find work and to sell the goods they grow or make.

Providing people with useful materials allows them to build businesses and homes for themselves.

Careers That Count: Knowing the Area

Humanitarian aid workers need to read about and spend time in the place where they are going to be working. This ensures that they better understand how the people there think and behave, and what matters to them. This helps aid workers figure out long-term plans that will really help people.

When aid workers organize farm animals for a family, that family can become self-sufficient and may not need to ask for aid again.

WHAT MAKES A GREAT HUMANITARIAN AID WORKER?

Aid workers have to be intelligent and good at **research**. Before they start a development project, they study different options. They then try out some of the options to see if they work before spending a lot of money on them. How do you think such a thoughtful approach helps aid workers achieve results that really count?

WORKING WITH CHILDREN

A lot of the work that aid workers do helps children. However, children have some particular needs and some aid workers specialize in working with children in need.

Children need food, water, family, and shelter. Once these basic needs are met, children need education. When people are poor, live far from schools, or have become refugees, children miss out on education. Some aid workers help set up schools and teach there or they train adults to be teachers. Some aid workers train older children with skills that will give them a better chance of getting a job. Children also need to play. Some aid workers, for example, in refugee camps, run centers where children can come to play. This helps them forget the troubled world outside for a while.

At schools, aid workers can give children an education and food.

WHAT MAKES A GREAT HUMANITARIAN AID WORKER?

Aid workers have to be **empathetic**. They need to be able to understand what people are going through to be able to persuade them to accept help. In a few places, some parents refuse to send their children to school because they need them to earn money for the family. How can being empathetic help aid workers make parents understand the importance of an education?

Aid workers can help children who have lost their parents and have to look after their brothers or sisters by themselves.

Careers That Count: Street Children

Some aid workers are trained to help street children. These are children who have no homes and live on the streets. Aid workers are trained to help those children trust them, so that they will accept assistance and food. The aid workers may also be able to find the children a new home and family.

RISKS AND REWARDS

Humanitarian aid workers face some risks. They may work in war zones or countries where there are natural disasters. They also work in places where there are diseases, health threats like dirty water, or insects that pass on diseases. Most aid workers may face discomfort. For example, they may have to live without electricity or hot and cold running water. However, aid workers are trained to care for themselves and work with other people and organizations that help them in times of any danger.

Aid workers have to consider the downsides of the job before accepting it. However, most believe that the rewards are worth the sacrifices. Most aid workers say that living and working in different countries can be fascinating and very exciting. Many say that on a good day, when things go right and they make someone's world a better place to live, it can be the best job in the world!

Aid workers help put smiles on the faces of children in need.

WHAT MAKES A GREAT HUMANITARIAN AID WORKER?

A great humanitarian aid worker is **dedicated** to the job. Aid workers give 100 percent effort to the job they do, because it can make the difference between life and death. Could you have the dedication it takes to be a humanitarian aid worker?

Aid work is not a nine-to-five job. Aid workers are often expected to work long hours and for no extra pay. They must be willing to work during their free time to learn more about the area where they are working, or to research ways of helping the community they are with.

Aid workers often work in difficult conditions to help people in need.

COULD YOU HAVE A CAREER THAT COUNTS?

Do you want to become a humanitarian aid worker? Following these steps will help you reach your goal.

Subjects to study at school:
You do not need to study particular subjects, but you need to be **informed** about the world. Geography, economics, religion, and sociology might be helpful subjects to take.

Work experience: Volunteer with charities and aid agencies on weekends and during vacations. Later on, do voluntary work at home and/or abroad to gain experience. Aid work is a difficult and important job, so most charities and aid agencies prefer to hire people who have experience before sending them into a situation where their decisions affect lives.

Qualifications: You will need to have a degree, and some people also get a master's degree that relates to humanitarian work. The type of degree you get depends on the type of aid work you want to do. For example, if you want to do medical aid work, you will need to get a degree in medicine or nursing.

Build your knowledge: Learn about humanitarian aid through books, articles, and websites. Learn about the different kinds of aid work that people do and what organizations employ aid workers. Make sure you are healthy and fit and take a first aid course, if you can.

Getting the job: Aid work is very competitive so you will need to have something special to make you stand out. If you apply for a job with an aid agency, make sure the experience you have gained is suitable for them.

GLOSSARY

abroad In a foreign country.

adaptable Being able to change in order to cope with a new situation.

applications Formal or official requests to someone who is in charge of something you want or need.

characteristics Features or qualities belonging to a particular person or thing.

charities Non-profit-making organizations set up to help people in need.

clinics Places where people can go to get medical treatment or advice.

communicator Someone who is good at giving and receiving information.

communities Groups of people living in the same place or who share a common interest.

crops Plants grown for food.

dedicated Devoted and completely committed to something.

development Improving something.

diagnose To figure out what is wrong with someone who is sick.

distribute To give out.

droughts Long periods of time when there is little or no rain.

economic development Making a community richer.

empathetic Having the ability to understand how another person feels.

famines Situations in which many people do not have enough food to eat.

financial To do with money.

first aid Help given to a sick or injured person until full medical treatment is available.

flee To run away from something.

headquarters Places where the people who control organizations work.

infections Diseases caused by germs.

informed To know a lot about something.

livelihoods Ways of earning money to live.

loans Money that is borrowed.

natural disasters Disasters caused by nature.

refugees People who have had to leave their country and are too afraid to go back.

research Study.

resources Things that are useful.

reunite To be joined with something or someone again.

sacrifices Giving up things that you want to keep.

sanitation The process of keeping places free from dirt.

self-sufficient Able to live without help or support from others.

shelter A structure, such as a house or tent, which protects people and things.

sociology The study of society (how people live and work together).

specialists People who have special knowledge and training to do a particular job.

starve To suffer or die from lack of food.

temporary Lasting for only a limited period of time.

vaccinations Putting vaccines into the human body, usually by injections.

vaccines Substances that protect against particular diseases.

volunteers People who work without being paid.

war zones Places where battles are being fought.

water pumps Devices for getting water from under the ground.

FURTHER READING

Lusted, Marcia Amidon. *Surviving Natural Disasters* (Shockzone – True Survival Stories). Minneapolis, MN: 21st Century Press, 2014.

Marsico, Katie. *Doctors Without Borders* (Community Connections: How Do They Help?). North Mankato, MN: Cherry Lake Publishing, 2014.

Morley, David. *Healing Our World: Inside Doctors Without Borders.* Brighton, MS: Fitzhenry and Whiteside, 2008.

Watts, Clare: *Natural Disasters* (DK Eyewitness Books). New York, NY: Dorling Kindersley, 2012.

WEBSITES

Due to the changing nature of Internet links, PowerKids Press has developed an online list of websites related to the subject of this book. This site is updated regularly. Please use this link to access the list: **www.powerkidslinks.com/ctc/haw**

INDEX